WALKING STICKS

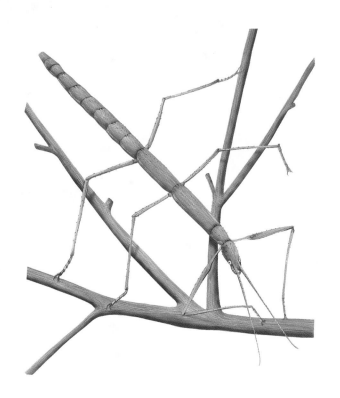

For a free color catalog describing Gareth Stevens' list of high-quality books and multimedia programs, call 1-800-542-2595 (USA) or 1-800-461-9120 (Canada). Gareth Stevens Publishing's Fax: (414) 225-0377. See our catalog, too, on the World Wide Web: http://gsinc.com

Library of Congress Cataloging-in-Publication Data

Green, Tamara, 1945-
    Walking sticks / by Tamara Green ; illustrated by Tony Gibbons.
       p. cm. -- (The New creepy crawly collection)
    Includes bibliographical references and index.
    Summary: Examines the anatomy, behavior, life cycle, and different kinds of walking sticks.
    ISBN 0-8368-1917-9 (lib. bdg.)
    1. Stick insects--Juvenile literature. [1. Stick insects.] I. Gibbons, Tony, ill.
II. Title. III. Series.
QL509.5.G74 1997
595.7'29--dc21   97-7332

This North American edition first published in 1997 by
Gareth Stevens Publishing
1555 North RiverCenter Drive, Suite 201
Milwaukee, Wisconsin 53212 USA

This U.S. edition © 1997 by Gareth Stevens, Inc. Created with original © 1996 by Quartz Editorial Services, 112 Station Road, Edgware HA8 7AQ U.K.

Additional illustrations by Clare Heronneau.

Consultant: Matthew Robertson, Senior Keeper, Bristol Zoo, Bristol, England.

Printed in Mexico

1 2 3 4 5 6 7 8 9 01 00 99 98 97

THE NEW

CREEPY CRAWLY
COLLECTION

WALKING STICKS

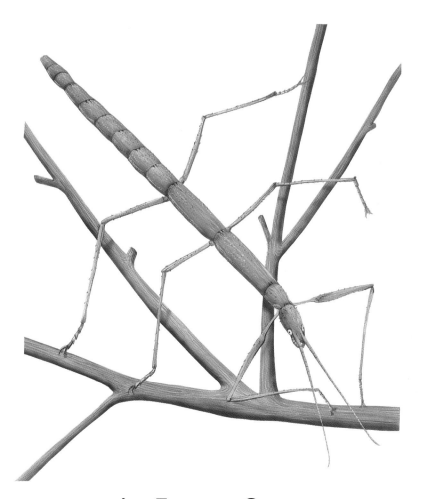

by Tamara Green
Illustrated by Tony Gibbons

Gareth Stevens Publishing
MILWAUKEE

Contents

5   Getting to know walking sticks

6   True to their name

8   Masters of disguise

10   Midnight feasts

12   Keeping walking sticks as pets

14   Birth of a walking stick

16   Lose a leg, grow a leg

18   Meet the family

20   Other great pretenders

22   Did you know?

24   Glossary
      Books and Videos
      Index

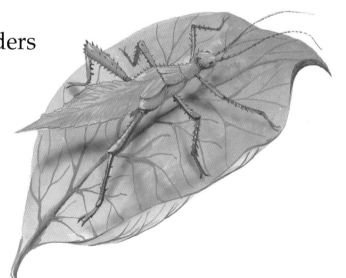

Getting to know walking sticks

They may not move around very much; they are not brightly colored; and they are usually completely silent. Yet walking sticks vary a lot and are fascinating to study, as you are about to discover. In fact, they can perform some of the most spectacular disappearing acts in the entire animal kingdom.

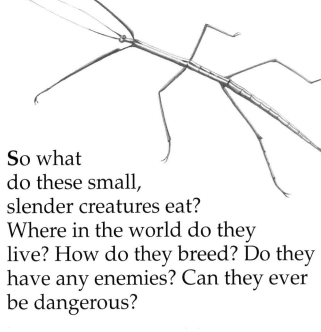

So what do these small, slender creatures eat? Where in the world do they live? How do they breed? Do they have any enemies? Can they ever be dangerous?

Read on and find out all about these experts of the art of camouflage.

Even if you keep walking sticks as pets, you may have to stare long and hard to find them in the foliage in their tank.

5

True to

Some walking sticks are very accurately named. That's because they look just like long, thin sticks. This is also the secret of their success. Walking sticks look so much like sticks, leaves, or twigs they are often entirely overlooked by predators.

Not only do their bodies look like vegetation, but their legs can also be held at angles so the limbs resemble offshoots. Stick insects are experts at camouflage — the ability to blend in with surroundings.

Take a look at the structure of a walking stick. At the top of the head are two long antennae.

These antennae are used for feeling the way ahead. The mouth, meanwhile, has surprisingly strong jaws for such a fragile-looking creature. The jaws are used for chewing on plants.

The walking stick's six legs (and wings, in some species) are attached to the thorax, behind which is the walking stick's abdomen.

their name

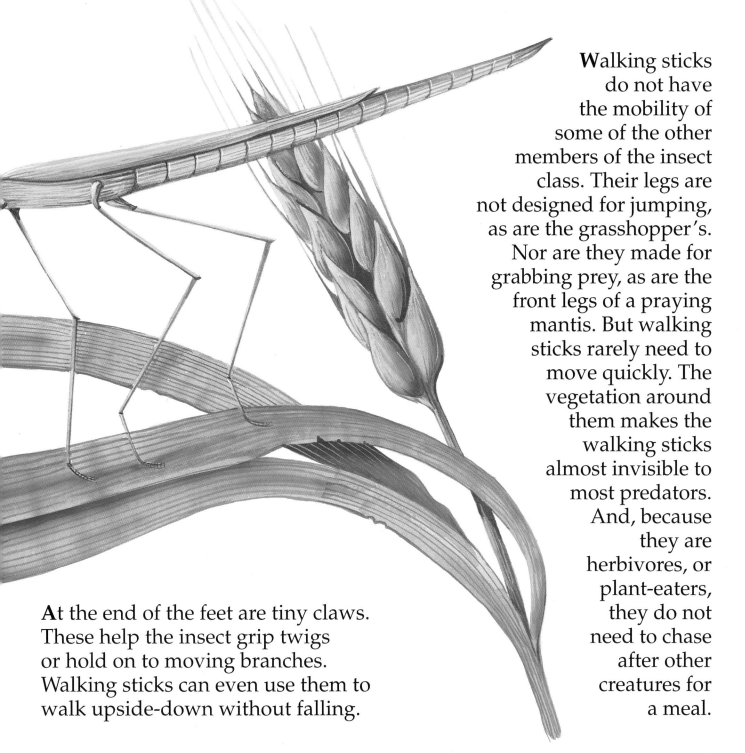

Walking sticks do not have the mobility of some of the other members of the insect class. Their legs are not designed for jumping, as are the grasshopper's. Nor are they made for grabbing prey, as are the front legs of a praying mantis. But walking sticks rarely need to move quickly. The vegetation around them makes the walking sticks almost invisible to most predators. And, because they are herbivores, or plant-eaters, they do not need to chase after other creatures for a meal.

At the end of the feet are tiny claws. These help the insect grip twigs or hold on to moving branches. Walking sticks can even use them to walk upside-down without falling.

Masters

Walking sticks are such superb masters of disguise that they often look just like the vegetation surrounding them, as you can see from the two very different types illustrated *below*. They have this ability to camouflage themselves right from the time they are born. Even their eggs look similar to plant seeds. Then, when one hatches on the ground, the emerging walking stick may be brown to match the fallen twigs and leaves around it. Later, as some of the insects climb up to fresh leaves, they can change to a shade of green. Other walking sticks are spotted and so may be very well hidden on tree bark.

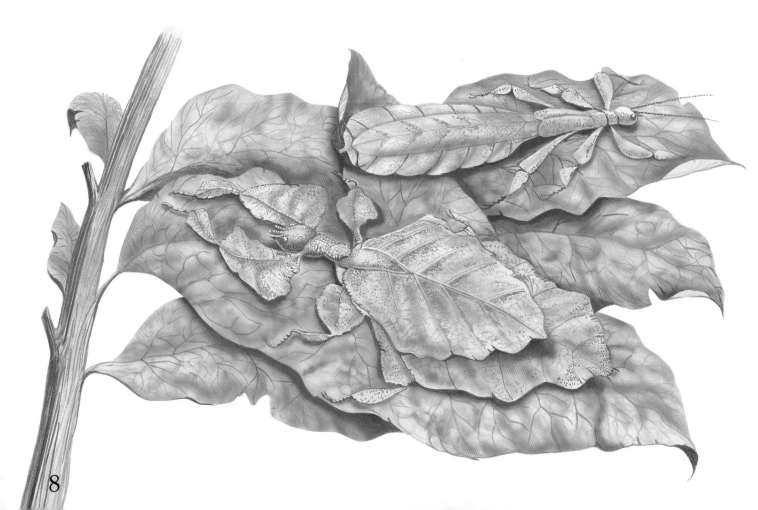

# of disguise

Even if the insects move a little from time to time, swaying from side to side, they will probably look just like thin twigs or leaves blowing in the breeze. The wings of walking sticks can sometimes be colorful, but the color usually remains hidden and shows only when the wings are unfolded for some reason. Scientists call this process "flash coloration," and it is useful for frightening off any would-be predators. You will need to look carefully to spot a walking stick in its natural environment. Remember, too, that a few species can even change color in the course of a single day.

Midnight

Walking sticks are creatures of the night, preferring to get plenty of rest during the day and then looking for food after sunset.

During daytime, they remain motionless, hiding among twigs or bark. If they are knocked off their branch, perhaps blown off by the wind, and drop to the ground, they will lie still wherever they land. They refuse to draw attention to themselves.

When darkness falls, walking sticks are ready to go looking for a midnight feast. They do not usually travel far for their meals and may even live on the very same plant that will form the main item in their diet for their entire lives.

Once they are moving, walking sticks are no longer so well camouflaged, so they are more vulnerable to attack. But, under cover of darkness, they are less likely to be noticed by a predator.

feasts

Keeping walking

Walking sticks are not often kept as pets because some of them are very difficult to keep. But walking sticks are also unique and can be fun to observe both in nature and in the home as pets.

You should be able to buy walking sticks from a pet shop or special breeder. It would be best to purchase them at the nymph stage after they have molted several times. Check that they have all their legs and that their bodies look healthy.

You can take walking sticks home in a plastic box with air holes in the lid and with some suitable plants inside. However, you will need a permanent dwelling for your stick insects. This could be an aquarium with a special top to provide good ventilation. Ask for advice from the person who sells you your new pets.

sticks as pets

Make sure the walking sticks have plenty of space. If they are over-crowded, they will not be able to feed properly and may start to fight.

Blackberry leaves will provide an ideal diet for most walking sticks, and some will eat rhododendron leaves. Keep these moist with a plant spray. Be sure to put twigs in the tank, too, so that your walking sticks have something to climb on. Some types of walking sticks like to drink, so you will need to give them fresh water regularly. But the dish must be shallow so they don't drown.

A paper floor covering will need to be changed a couple of times each week to keep the tank clean. Look after your walking sticks properly, and they should live their full life-span. If you're lucky, they might even lay eggs and provide you with a new generation of walking sticks.

Birth of a

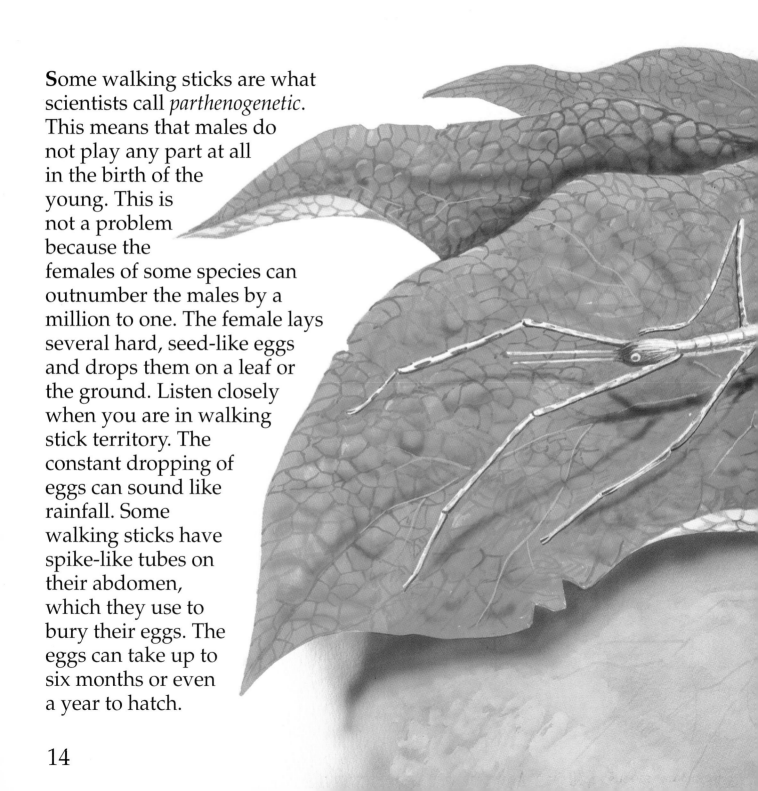

Some walking sticks are what scientists call *parthenogenetic*. This means that males do not play any part at all in the birth of the young. This is not a problem because the females of some species can outnumber the males by a million to one. The female lays several hard, seed-like eggs and drops them on a leaf or the ground. Listen closely when you are in walking stick territory. The constant dropping of eggs can sound like rainfall. Some walking sticks have spike-like tubes on their abdomen, which they use to bury their eggs. The eggs can take up to six months or even a year to hatch.

walking stick

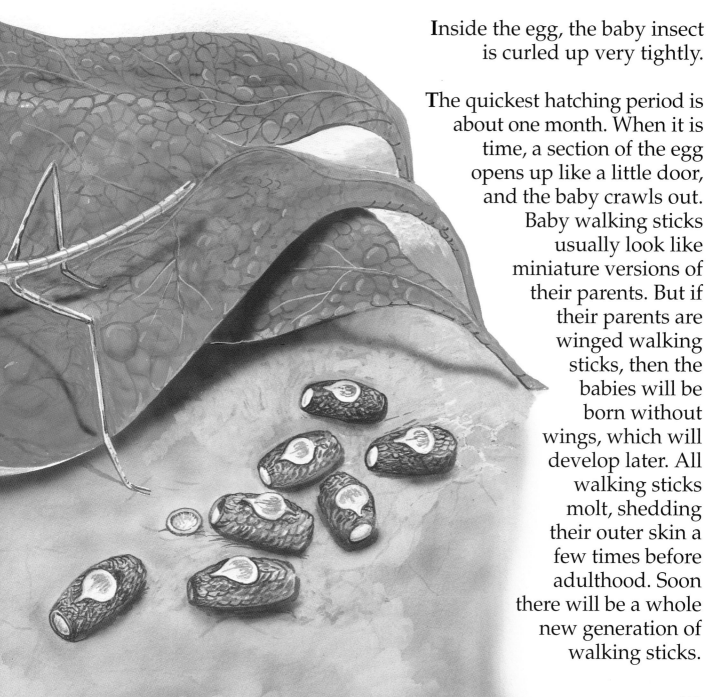

Inside the egg, the baby insect is curled up very tightly.

The quickest hatching period is about one month. When it is time, a section of the egg opens up like a little door, and the baby crawls out. Baby walking sticks usually look like miniature versions of their parents. But if their parents are winged walking sticks, then the babies will be born without wings, which will develop later. All walking sticks molt, shedding their outer skin a few times before adulthood. Soon there will be a whole new generation of walking sticks.

15

Lose a leg,

The hungry leaf mantis, although a relative of walking sticks, was tempted by the idea of a walking stick meal. The mantis was very hungry.

But if some types of walking sticks are threatened, they will do all they can to protect themselves. Even though most are not aggressive, they do have a few self-defense tricks up their sleeve.

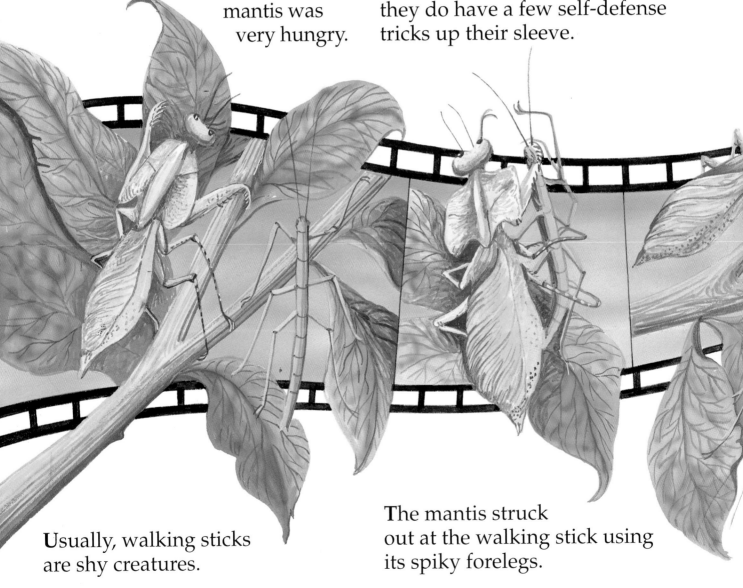

Usually, walking sticks are shy creatures.

The mantis struck out at the walking stick using its spiky forelegs.

grow a leg

The leaf mantis now grabbed one of the walking stick's legs. Thinking it had a good grip on its prey, it prepared to feast. But the walking stick had a secret line of defense. It had a method, using special

The leaf mantis had been well camouflaged and almost invisible before it started moving. But now, a small monkey was alerted and leaped out at it. It would make a delicious snack.

muscles, of severing its own leg, which came away in the mantis' grasp.

The battle was not yet over, however, even though the walking stick lay still.

Luckily, the monkey did not notice the walking stick, only the leaf mantis. The young walking stick's severed limb would soon grow back. But until then, it would have to manage with just five legs.

Meet the

There are lots of walking sticks, and they all belong to a group of insects scientists call *Phasmida*, a word that comes from the Latin for "ghost." What a good name for insects that are so difficult to see! The laboratory walking stick, *below*, originated in India and is a popular pet. It rarely moves during the day and requires little space in which to live. Laboratory walking sticks are almost all females and will lay large numbers of eggs without the help of a male.

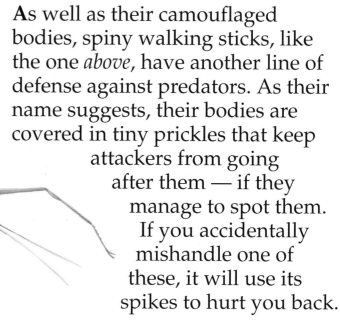

As well as their camouflaged bodies, spiny walking sticks, like the one *above*, have another line of defense against predators. As their name suggests, their bodies are covered in tiny prickles that keep attackers from going after them — if they manage to spot them. If you accidentally mishandle one of these, it will use its spikes to hurt you back.

family

A jungle-dweller, the Costa Rican walking stick, *right*, is slim and a dark shade of brown, with two white stripes all along the body. The females may be up to 6 inches (15 centimeters) long, but the males are a lot smaller. Their coloring is ideal for camouflage on the jungle floor.

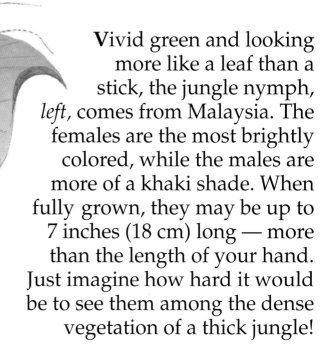

Vivid green and looking more like a leaf than a stick, the jungle nymph, *left*, comes from Malaysia. The females are the most brightly colored, while the males are more of a khaki shade. When fully grown, they may be up to 7 inches (18 cm) long — more than the length of your hand. Just imagine how hard it would be to see them among the dense vegetation of a thick jungle!

Other great

Walking sticks are not the only creatures with a remarkable ability to hide themselves from danger. Bark bugs from Central America, *right*, for example, will disguise themselves by resting on the bark of trees. Only the sharpest eye can detect them, since their coloring exactly matches the color of the bark. Some types are even transparent, which makes them even harder to see.

Most katydids, like the one *below*, have a grayish-brown or green coloring. This helps them blend into the background when they sit on tree bark or foliage. Some can even fold their wings so they look just like dead leaves.

Some katydid wings may also have veins that resemble the markings on leaves. When on the ground, katydids can easily camouflage themselves among fallen twigs, too.

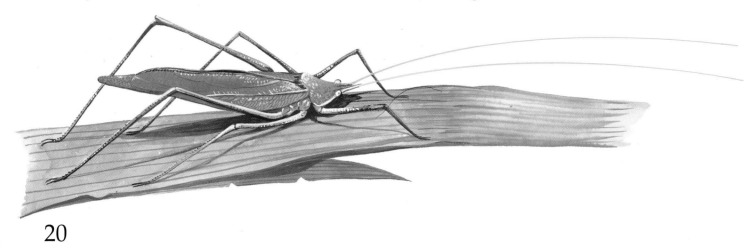

pretenders

Beetles, meanwhile, are also very successful at disguising themselves. Many hide among twigs and branches that are covered in moss or lichen, with coloring that matches their own. Others resemble dangerous insects in order to discourage predators. The British wasp beetle, *right*, for example, has black and yellow stripes and is often mistaken for a wasp by its enemies.

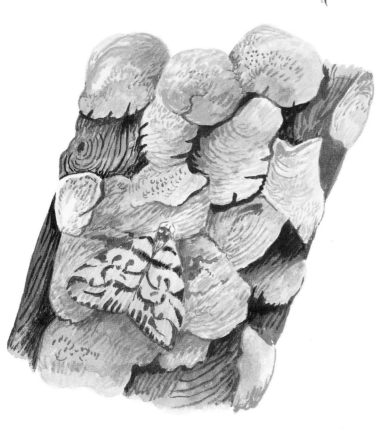

Lots of moths, too, conceal their bodies very successfully against tree bark. As you can see *left*, the wings of this particular moth blend in perfectly with its background, and it is almost invisible. This keeps it safe from danger. In response to the threat posed by predators, many other moths have also developed special wing patterns that act as a useful form of camouflage.

Did you know?

How many types of walking sticks are there in the world?
Walking sticks belong to an order of insects called *Phasmida*. This group contains thousands of types of walking sticks and leaf insects.

▼ Do any creatures want to eat walking sticks?
Bats, like the one shown here, birds, monkeys, small mammals, and lizards are among the most dangerous predators faced by walking sticks.

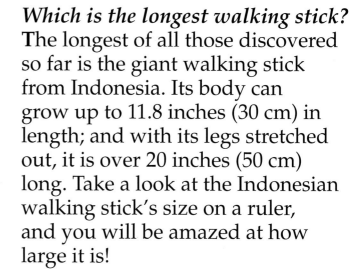

Which is the longest walking stick?
The longest of all those discovered so far is the giant walking stick from Indonesia. Its body can grow up to 11.8 inches (30 cm) in length; and with its legs stretched out, it is over 20 inches (50 cm) long. Take a look at the Indonesian walking stick's size on a ruler, and you will be amazed at how large it is!

Can walking sticks fly?
A few types of walking sticks do have wings and can fly, but most do not. Flying stick insects can hide their wings when they are resting, so it is surprising when they eventually fly off.

Do walking sticks make a noise?
Most walking sticks are silent. Even when they eat, they do so very quietly. But one of their relatives, the jungle nymph from Malaysia, makes a hissing sound with its wings if it is attacked.

Are walking sticks fussy about food?

Some types are very particular and will only eat certain leaves. If you buy any as pets, be sure to get some advice from the pet shop.

How should you handle a walking stick?

Walking sticks need very careful handling because they are delicate. If you place a finger in front of them, they may start to walk on your hand. Large ones can be picked up if you hold them gently on both sides of the thorax. Do not press hard. You will need to remove them very gently from a plant to avoid damaging their legs. Some, such as the jungle nymph, have sharp spines and powerful legs, and will draw blood if handled roughly.

Can walking sticks be harmful?

If there are too many walking sticks in one area, they can cause damage to their natural habitat. They may devastate woodland areas, for example, by eating all the plants. A few species also have glands that emit a nasty-smelling liquid. If this comes in contact with your eyes, it may cause painful swelling and even temporary blindness.

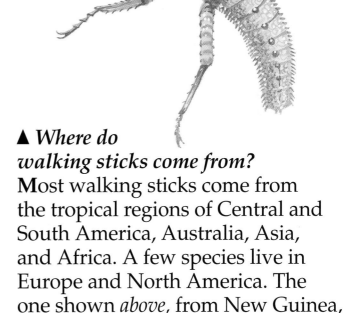

▲ Where do walking sticks come from?

Most walking sticks come from the tropical regions of Central and South America, Australia, Asia, and Africa. A few species live in Europe and North America. The one shown *above*, from New Guinea, is the giant spiny walking stick.

How can you tell a male walking stick from a female?

In the winged species, males generally have bigger wings than females. The females, however, are usually plumper than the males. In females, you can also sometimes spot the egg-laying organ that scientists call the ovipositor.

23

Glossary

abdomen — one of the three main body parts of an insect. The walking stick's abdomen is behind the thorax and contains the stomach.

antennae — thin, movable sense organs on an insect's head that are used for smelling, feeling, and tasting.

aquarium — a glass container commonly used as a home for fish. Walking sticks can also live in an aquarium if properly ventilated.

camouflage — a disguise that helps plants, animals, and humans blend in with their natural surroundings.

molt — to shed an outer covering or skin.

nymph — a young insect that resembles an adult but is smaller.

parthenogenesis — a reproductive process in which a female of a species is able to have babies without needing to mate with a male.

predators — animals that kill and eat other animals. Bats, birds, monkeys, and lizards are some of the walking stick's main predators.

thorax — the central section of an insect's body, which houses the heart.

Books and Videos

Amazing Insects. Laurence Mound (Knopf Books for Young Readers)

Flying Insects. WINGS series. Patricia Lantier-Sampon (Gareth Stevens)

Insects. Philip Steele (Watts)

Stick Insects. Barrie Watts (Watts)

Insect Disguises. (Altschul Group video)

Insects: The Little Things That Run the World. (Wood Knapp Video)

Index

antennae 6

bark bugs 20
British wasp beetles 21

Costa Rican walking sticks 19

flash coloration 9

giant spiny walking sticks 23
grasshoppers 7

herbivores 7

Indonesian giant walking sticks 22

jungle nymphs 19, 22, 23

katydids 20

laboratory walking sticks 18
leaf mantis 16, 17

moths 21

ovipositor 23

parthenogenetic 14
praying mantis 7
predators 6, 7, 9, 10, 18, 21, 22
prey 7, 17

spiny walking sticks 18

thorax 6, 23

walking sticks: and camouflage 5, 6, 7, 8-9, 10, 17, 18, 19, 20, 21; eating habits of 6, 7, 10-11, 13, 23; and flying 22; legs of 6, 7, 12, 16-17, 22, 23; and molting 12, 15; as pets 5, 12-13, 23; physical characteristics of 6-7; and reproduction 14-15, 18; and self-defense 16, 17, 18; sizes of 19, 22